W9-BAL-016

PLAYTALES

SLEEPING BEAUTY

MOIRA BUTTERFIELD

Heinemann Interactive Library
Des Plaines, Illinois

784034/

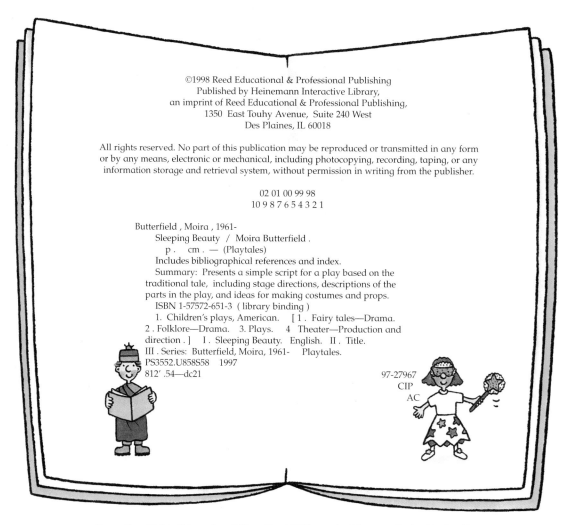

©1998 Reed Educational & Professional Publishing
Published by Heinemann Interactive Library,
an imprint of Reed Educational & Professional Publishing,
1350 East Touhy Avenue, Suite 240 West
Des Plaines, IL 60018

All rights reserved. No part of this publication may be reproduced or transmitted in any form or by any means, electronic or mechanical, including photocopying, recording, taping, or any information storage and retrieval system, without permission in writing from the publisher.

02 01 00 99 98
10 9 8 7 6 5 4 3 2 1

Butterfield , Moira , 1961-
    Sleeping Beauty / Moira Butterfield .
        p .   cm . — (Playtales)
    Includes bibliographical references and index.
    Summary: Presents a simple script for a play based on the traditional tale, including stage directions, descriptions of the parts in the play, and ideas for making costumes and props.
    ISBN 1-57572-651-3 (library binding)
    1. Children's plays, American.   [1 . Fairy tales—Drama.
2 . Folklore—Drama.   3. Plays.   4 Theater—Production and direction .]   I . Sleeping Beauty. English. II . Title.
III . Series: Butterfield, Moira, 1961-   Playtales.
PS3552.U858S58   1997
812' .54—dc21

97-27967
CIP
AC

Co-author: Robin Edwards • Editor: David Riley • Art Director: Cathy Tincknell • Designer: Anne Sharples • Photography: Trever Clifford • Illustrator: Sue Cony
Props: Anne Sharples

Thanks to: Jessie Croome, Natalie Walsh, Juliet Taylor and Christopher Liu:
Elisabeth Smith Model Agency

Printed and bound in Italy

You will need to use scissors and glue to make the props for your play. Always make sure an adult is there to help you.

Use only water-based face paints and makeup. Children with sensitive skin should use makeup and face paints with caution.

Contents

4 • Choose a Part
5 • Reading the Play
6 • Things to Make
9 • Stage and Sounds
10 • The Play

THE STORY OF SLEEPING BEAUTY

When a Bad Fairy puts a spell on Sleeping Beauty, it looks as if all will be lost. The poor Princess must stay asleep for one hundred years along with everyone else in her palace, until a handsome Prince rides by and saves the day with a kiss.

Choose a Part

This play is a story that you can read with your friends and perhaps even act out in front of an audience. You need up to four people. Before you start, choose which parts you would like to play.

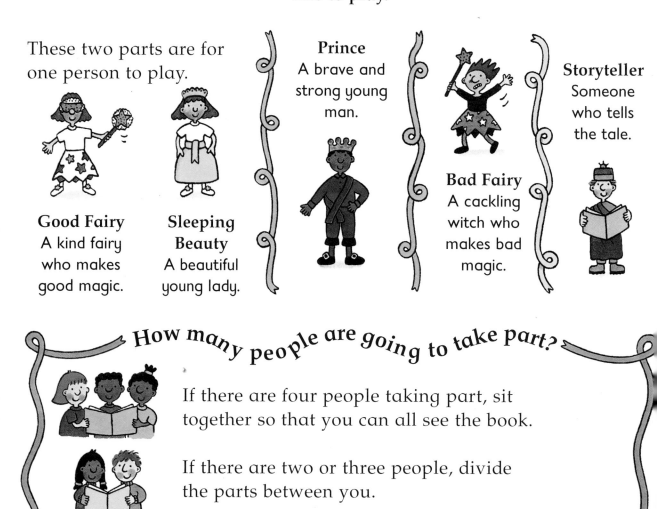

These two parts are for one person to play.

Good Fairy
A kind fairy who makes good magic.

Sleeping Beauty
A beautiful young lady.

Prince
A brave and strong young man.

Bad Fairy
A cackling witch who makes bad magic.

Storyteller
Someone who tells the tale.

How many people are going to take part?

If there are four people taking part, sit together so that you can all see the book.

If there are two or three people, divide the parts between you.

If you want to read the play on your own, use a different sounding voice for each part.

Reading the Play

Prince   **Sleeping Beauty**   **Storyteller**   **Good Fairy**   **Bad Fairy**

The play is made up of different lines. Next to each line there is a name and a picture. This shows who should be talking.

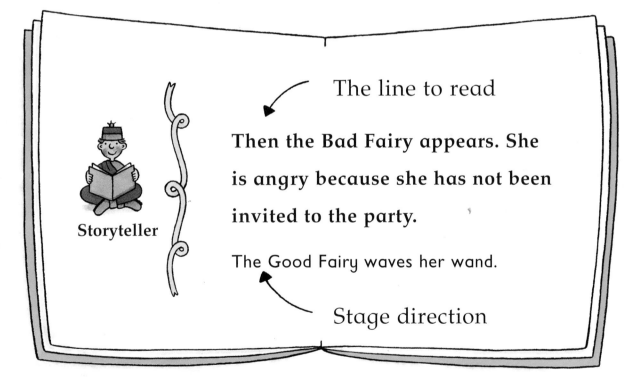

The line to read

Storyteller

Then the Bad Fairy appears. She is angry because she has not been invited to the party.

The Good Fairy waves her wand.

Stage direction

In between the lines there are some stage directions. They are suggestions for things you might do, such as, acting something out.

Things to Make

Here are some suggestions for costumes.

THE BAD FAIRY: CLOTHES AND PROPS

Wear a black T-shirt or a leotard with black tights and shoes. Make a black skirt and wand. Mess up your hair and add some scary face paint.

Make a Black Skirt
You need:
- A black trash bag
- Enough string or black ribbon to tie around your waist in a bow
- Scissors, ruler, and glue
- Gold and blue paper

1. Snip raggedly along the bottom of the trash bag to open it up.

2. Cut slits all around the top of the trash bag, about 3 in. down from the edge. Thread the string or ribbon through the slits.

3. Glue some blue and gold paper stars onto the skirt. Then pull the ends of the string tightly around your waist and tie them in a bow.

To disguise yourself at the spinning wheel (see page 16), wrap a shawl around you or a blanket to look like a cloak.

Face Painting Ideas
Paint green cheeks and a black wart. Put on dark lipstick and paint lots of big eyelashes or bushy eyebrows. Use hair gel to make your hair look wild and messy.

Make a Wand
You need:
- Black cardboard
- Scissors and glue
- Pencil and ruler
- Glitter or shiny paint
- Small plate

1. Cut two long thin handles about the same size as a ruler, from the cardboard. Glue them back-to-back to make your wand really strong.

2. Draw and cut out a star shape. To make it look even, draw a circle around a small plate, and then draw your star inside the circle.

3. Glue the star to the handle and decorate it with glitter or paint.

PRINCE: CLOTHES AND PROPS

Wear a grand crown and carry a sword to cut down the magic forest. Wear a dark blue shirt, and pants tucked into long blue socks. Put elegant cuffs around your knees and fancy buckles on your shoes.

Make a Crown
You need:
- Shiny cardboard (or plain cardboard that you can paint yellow to look like gold)
- Glue, pencil and scissors
- Tape measure and ruler
- Colored paper

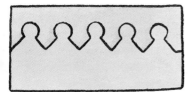

1. Draw a crown pattern on the back of the cardboard. It can be as wide as you like with points along the top. It should be 3 in. longer than the measurement around your head.

2. Cut out the shape and glue on scraps of colored paper.

3. Put the two ends together, overlapping by about 1 1/2 in. Check that it fits you and then tape or glue the ends together.

Cut out two cardboard buckle shapes and fix them to your shoes with barrettes.

Make a sword out of cardboard and paint it.

Make Knee Cuffs
You need:
- Black cardboard or thick paper
- Hole punch
- String or shoe-laces
- Ruler, pencil, and scissors
- Dinner plate

1. Draw part of the way around the dinner plate to make a curve with ends roughly 9 in. apart.

2. Go around the curve measuring 4 in. outward and making pencil marks all around it. Connect the marks to make a bigger curve.

Make two cuffs the same.

3. Cut out the shape and punch holes in the corners. Thread string through the holes as shown, and tie the cuffs together at the back of your legs.

7

GOOD FAIRY/SLEEPING BEAUTY: CLOTHES AND PROPS

Start off as the Good Fairy with a skirt just like the Bad Fairy's, but made with a white trash bag. Make a mask and wear a white T-shirt and white shoes. Wave a wand like the Bad Fairy's but decorated differently.

Change into Sleeping Beauty: Take off the mask and white skirt. Put on a party dress or a net skirt and a pretty tiara.

Make a Mask
You need:
- Some scrap paper and some stiff paper or thin cardboard
- Scissors, pencil, ruler, and glue
- Two long lengths of string
- Scraps of colored paper or paint for decoration

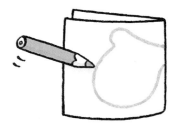

1. Practice first by cutting a rectangle of scrap paper 7 in. x 3 in. Fold it in half and draw a round shape up to the fold, as shown.

2. Cut around the shape and unfold the paper. Hold it to your face to check the size and mark where the eye-holes should be. Then cut them out.

3. Once you are happy with your practice mask, use it as a model to cut one from stiff paper or thin cardboard. Decorate it as you like.

4. Make a hole in each side and knot the strings through as shown. Tie them in a bow at the back.

Make a Net Skirt
You need:
- Piece of colored net 6 ft. wide and as long as the measurement from your waist to your feet
- Scissors and ruler
- 5 ft. of ribbon

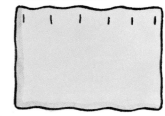

1. Lay the net flat and cut some slits all around the top, about 3 in. down from the edge.

2. Thread the ribbon through the slits and pull the skirt tight around your waist. Tie the ends in a bow.

Stage and Sounds

Once you have read the play through, you may want to perform it in front of an audience. If so, read through this section first. Rehearse the play, working out when you are going to come on and off stage and what actions you are going to perform.

PROPS

Wrap a doll in a sheet and use it to represent Sleeping Beauty at the Christening.

You will need a chair or a stool for the Bad Fairy to sit on when she spins. She needs a shawl.

When Sleeping Beauty is asleep, she could sit on a chair or lie on a quilt, or on some floor cushions.

The Bad Fairy needs to pretend to be sitting beside a spinning wheel. She could wrap a circle of lengths of wool around her hands to represent this.

Sleeping Beauty should practice pretending to prick her finger on an imaginary point.

SOUNDS

Riding noise:

As the Prince rides in, someone offstage should make a clip-clopping noise by banging two coconut halves together or tapping a metal ruler on a door. If you have neither, experiment with different objects to get a good noise that the audience will hear.

LIGHTING

If you perform at night in a lit room, you can create an exciting effect by asking an assistant to flicker a flashlight quickly off and then on again as the Bad Fairy does her spell.

REHEARSING

Rehearse the play before you ask someone to watch.

The Play

Storyteller

Once upon a time, long ago, a King and Queen lived in a beautiful palace surrounded by gardens. One day the Queen gave birth to a baby Princess. On the day of her christening, the King held a big party at the palace. The guest of honor was the Good Fairy, who gave the Princess some magic gifts.

The Storyteller points to the Good Fairy, who is holding a baby doll. The Fairy waves her wand over the doll.

Good Fairy

Sweet little one, I wish for you
love and laughter ... wisdom, too.
beauty, kindness, gentle ways,
and happiness through all your days.

Storyteller

The Good Fairy had an enemy, the mean nasty
Bad Fairy! The King had not invited her to the
christening, but she came anyway.

Bad Fairy

So! You're having a party and you didn't invite me! You're going to be very sorry.

Good Fairy

Please don't harm the Princess.

Bad Fairy

Oh be quiet, goody-goody. I'm going to give the Princess a little magic gift of my own...

The Bad Fairy points her wand at the baby doll.

Bad Fairy

On your sixteenth birthday, you will prick your finger on a spinning wheel.
Then you will die!

The Bad Fairy laughs a nasty witch's laugh and disappears.

Storyteller

The Bad Fairy's spell was very powerful and could not be completely broken. The Good Fairy could only change it.

The Good Fairy waves her wand over the baby doll.

Good Fairy

On the eve of your sixteenth birthday you will not die. Instead, you will fall into a deep sleep for one hundred years.

COSTUME CHANGE

The Good Fairy should now change into her Sleeping Beauty outfit.

13

Storyteller

The King tried his best to stop the Bad Fairy from getting her way. He had all the spinning wheels in his kingdom chopped up and burned.

Storyteller

As the years passed, the Princess grew into a beautiful young woman.

The Storyteller points to Sleeping Beauty, who twirls around to show how beautiful she is.

Storyteller: On the eve of her sixteenth birthday, she took a walk through the palace...

Sleeping Beauty: It's my birthday tomorrow! I'm so excited I can't sit still. Wait a minute ... I've never seen this door before. I wonder where it leads?

Make a creaking noise as Sleeping Beauty pretends to open the door.

Storyteller: The door was a magic trick. Behind it were some magic stairs. At the top, there was a magic room, and sitting in the magic room was the Bad Fairy!

The Bad Fairy sits on a chair with a shawl or cloak to hide her costume. She pretends to be spinning (see page 9).

Bad Fairy
(in old lady voice)

Hello, dearie. Come in and see the lovely wool on the spinning wheel. Come closer ... closer ... Don't be scared.

Sleeping Beauty walks slowly towards the Bad Fairy, as if she is hypnotized.

Bad Fairy
(in old lady voice)

Go on, dearie. Touch it ... Touch it ...

Sleeping Beauty reaches out. She appears to touch a sharp point and prick her finger.

Sleeping Beauty

Aaaah! My finger!

Bad Fairy

Now my evil spell is complete!

The Bad Fairy throws off her shawl or cloak and disappears, laughing wickedly.

Sleeping Beauty faints and lies still as if in a deep sleep (see page 9 for prop idea).

Storyteller

So, the Bad Fairy's spell had come true, except for one thing. The Princess was not dead, she was just asleep. So was everyone else in the palace ... the servants, the footmen, the cooks, even the King and Queen.

Get everyone taking part to make snoring noises.

Storyteller

Time passed, day after day, year after year ... and a great thick forest grew up around the palace full of sleeping people. Exactly one hundred years later, a Prince came riding by.

Make a riding noise (see page 9).

What a strange place. It looks as if no one has ever been able to get through these tangled trees. I think I'll try with my trusty sword.

Prince

The Prince raises his sword and appears to hack and chop his way through the forest. Then he stands back and gasps.

These trees are magic! They're moving apart for me. Wow! There's a palace in the middle!

Prince

19

Make a knocking noise on the back of your book.

Prince

> Hello, is anyone there...? No one seems to be guarding the palace door. I'll go inside.

The other performers should make some snoring noises (offstage if there is an audience).

Prince

> The palace guards are snoring! My goodness, a King and Queen are fast asleep on their thrones! Now which way shall I go ...?

Storyteller

The Prince went this way and that, exploring the palace.

He finds Sleeping Beauty.

Prince

Who's this? She sleeps so gently. I've never seen anyone so beautiful.

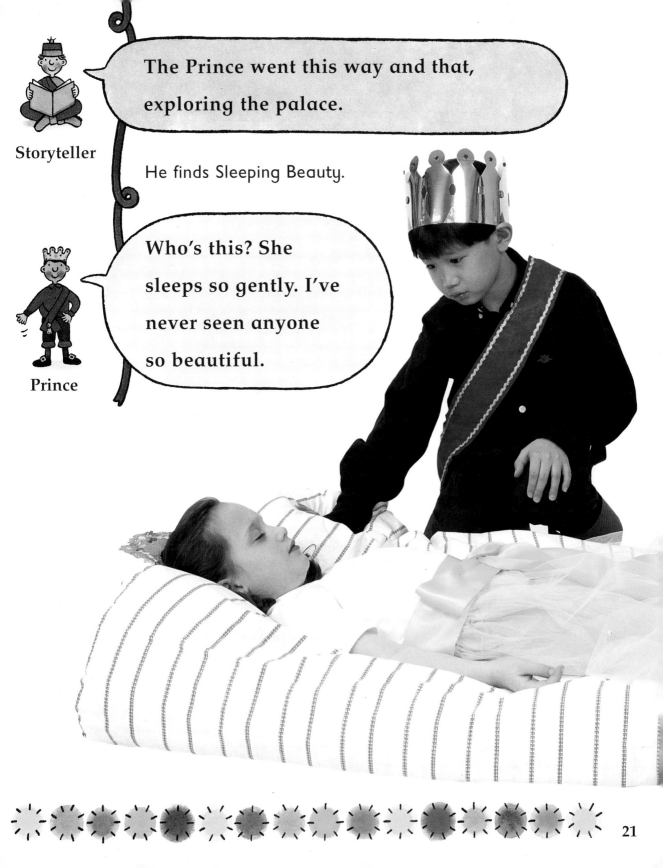

21

The Prince bends over and kisses Sleeping Beauty, who slowly awakens.

Sleeping Beauty

> What's happening? I must be dreaming.
>
> Who are you? Where am I?

Prince

> Don't be frightened. I think you've
> woken from a deep, deep sleep.

Sleeping Beauty

I think I remember. There was a wicked fairy and a spinning wheel and bad magic ...

Prince

You're safe now, my beautiful lady. I will never let anyone harm you again.

Storyteller

Then everybody in the palace woke up. Life began once again, and very soon the Prince and Princess fell in love and were married.

Sleeping Beauty and the Prince hold hands.

Sleeping Beauty

The Bad Fairy's spell is broken.

Prince

Let's have a wedding day.

Storyteller

Now everyone is happy. We can end our little play.

Finish the play by bowing to each other or to the audience.